LOOK INSIDE
CROSS-SECTIONS
PLANES

ILLUSTRATED BY
HANS JENSSEN

WRITTEN BY
MICHAEL JOHNSTONE

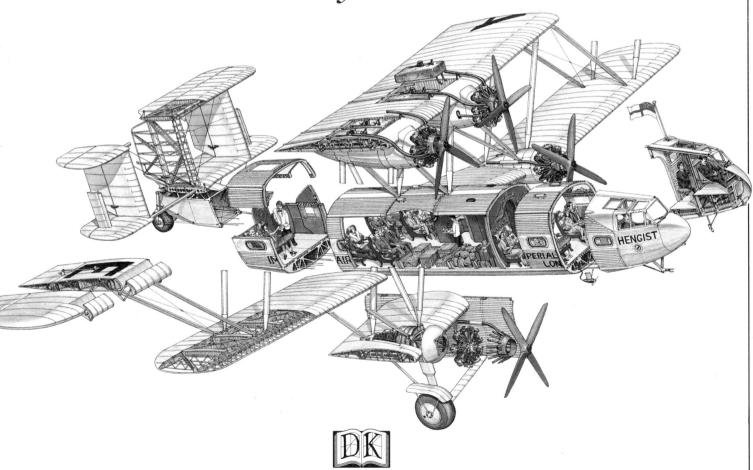

DK

DORLING KINDERSLEY
LONDON • NEW YORK • STUTTGART

A DORLING KINDERSLEY BOOK

Art Editor Dorian Spencer Davies
Designer Sharon Grant
Senior Art Editor C. David Gillingwater
Senior Editor John C. Miles
Production Ruth Cobb
Consultant Andrew Nahum
The Science Museum

First published in 1994
by Dorling Kindersley Limited,
9 Henrietta Street, London WC2E 8PS

A CIP catalogue record for this book is available
from the British Library

ISBN 07513-5164-4

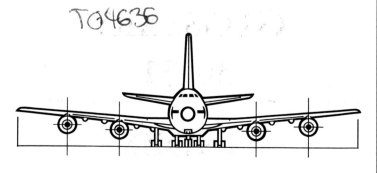

Reproduced by Dot Gradations, Essex
Printed and bound by Proost, Belgium

CONTENTS

TRIPLANE
6-7

HANDLEY PAGE
8-9

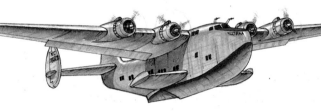

BOEING 314
10-11

SPITFIRE
12-13

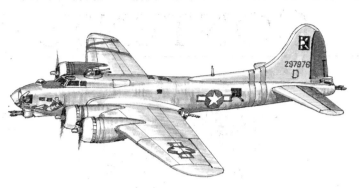

FLYING FORTRESS
14-15

HARRIER
24-25

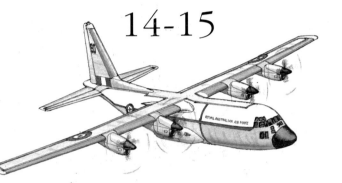

HERCULES
16-17 / 18-19

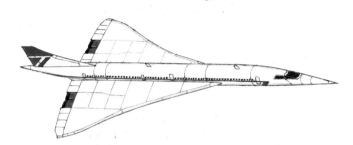

CONCORDE
26-27

BOEING 747
20-21

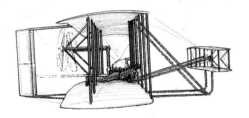

TIMELINE
28-29

GLOSSARY
30-31

PIPER CHIEFTAIN
22-23

INDEX
32

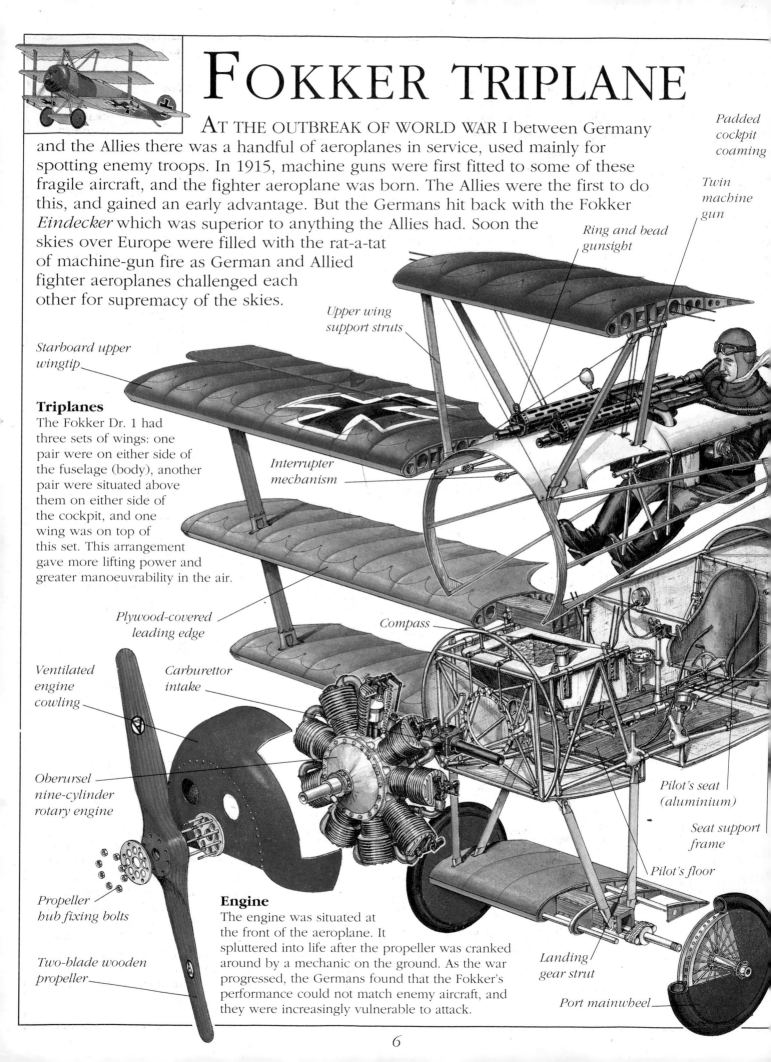

FOKKER TRIPLANE

AT THE OUTBREAK OF WORLD WAR I between Germany and the Allies there was a handful of aeroplanes in service, used mainly for spotting enemy troops. In 1915, machine guns were first fitted to some of these fragile aircraft, and the fighter aeroplane was born. The Allies were the first to do this, and gained an early advantage. But the Germans hit back with the Fokker *Eindecker* which was superior to anything the Allies had. Soon the skies over Europe were filled with the rat-a-tat of machine-gun fire as German and Allied fighter aeroplanes challenged each other for supremacy of the skies.

Padded cockpit coaming

Twin machine gun

Ring and bead gunsight

Upper wing support struts

Starboard upper wingtip

Triplanes

The Fokker Dr. 1 had three sets of wings: one pair were on either side of the fuselage (body), another pair were situated above them on either side of the cockpit, and one wing was on top of this set. This arrangement gave more lifting power and greater manoeuvrability in the air.

Interrupter mechanism

Plywood-covered leading edge

Compass

Ventilated engine cowling

Carburettor intake

Oberursel nine-cylinder rotary engine

Pilot's seat (aluminium)

Seat support frame

Pilot's floor

Propeller hub fixing bolts

Engine

The engine was situated at the front of the aeroplane. It spluttered into life after the propeller was cranked around by a mechanic on the ground. As the war progressed, the Germans found that the Fokker's performance could not match enemy aircraft, and they were increasingly vulnerable to attack.

Two-blade wooden propeller

Landing gear strut

Port mainwheel

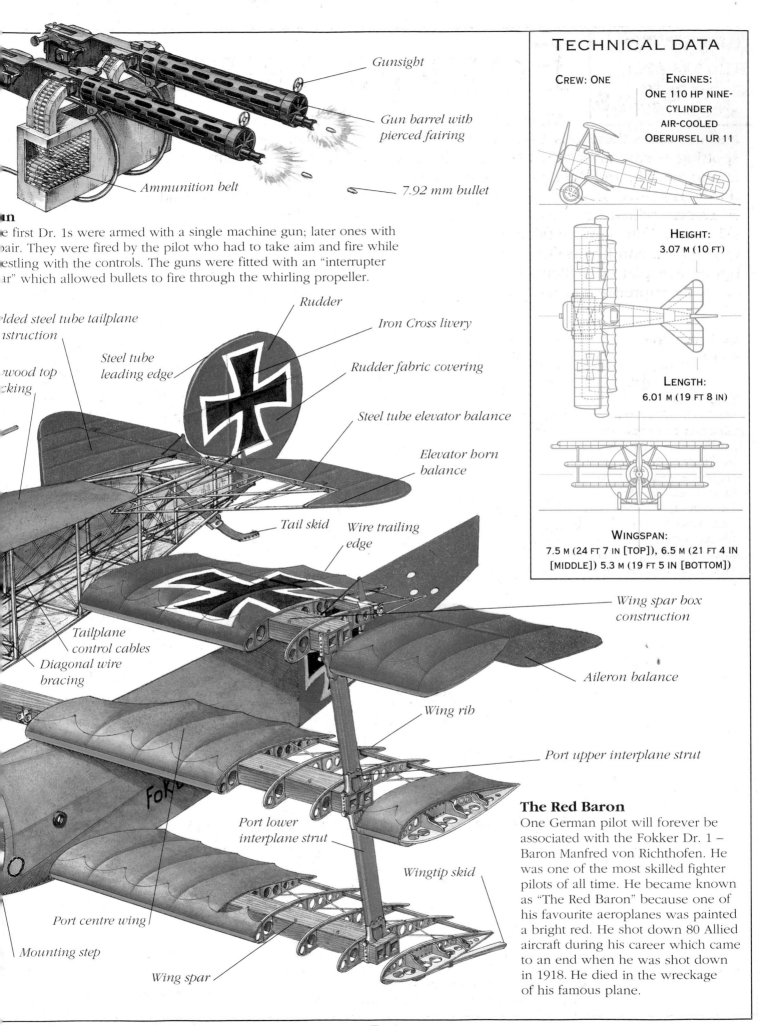

Gunsight

Gun barrel with pierced fairing

Ammunition belt

7.92 mm bullet

...un

...e first Dr. 1s were armed with a single machine gun; later ones with ...air. They were fired by the pilot who had to take aim and fire while ...estling with the controls. The guns were fitted with an "interrupter ...ar" which allowed bullets to fire through the whirling propeller.

Rudder

Iron Cross livery

...lded steel tube tailplane ...nstruction

...wood top ...cking

Steel tube leading edge

Rudder fabric covering

Steel tube elevator balance

Elevator horn balance

Tail skid

Wire trailing edge

Tailplane control cables

Diagonal wire bracing

Wing spar box construction

Aileron balance

Wing rib

Port upper interplane strut

Port lower interplane strut

Wingtip skid

Port centre wing

Mounting step

Wing spar

TECHNICAL DATA

CREW: ONE

ENGINES:
ONE 110 HP NINE-
CYLINDER
AIR-COOLED
OBERURSEL UR 11

HEIGHT:
3.07 M (10 FT)

LENGTH:
6.01 M (19 FT 8 IN)

WINGSPAN:
7.5 M (24 FT 7 IN [TOP]), 6.5 M (21 FT 4 IN
[MIDDLE]) 5.3 M (19 FT 5 IN [BOTTOM])

The Red Baron

One German pilot will forever be associated with the Fokker Dr. 1 – Baron Manfred von Richthofen. He was one of the most skilled fighter pilots of all time. He became known as "The Red Baron" because one of his favourite aeroplanes was painted a bright red. He shot down 80 Allied aircraft during his career which came to an end when he was shot down in 1918. He died in the wreckage of his famous plane.

HANDLEY PAGE

ONLY EIGHT HANDLEY PAGE H.P. 42s were built between 1930 and 1931, but by the time they went out of service in 1940, they had flown great distances and had earned a place in the affection of crew and passengers alike. They were, in the words of their manufacturer, "the world's first airliners". Many of the passengers they carried said they were the most comfortable planes they ever flew in. Four H.P. 42s carried mail and passengers between Cairo, Egypt, and Karachi (then in India). The other four flew between London, England and Paris, France. All were given "H" names – Hannibal, Hadrian, Hanno, and Horsa were the eastern planes. Hercules, Horatius, Hengist, and Helena flew in Europe.

Wings

In order to give the passengers an uninterrupted view of the ground below, the lower wings were fitted to the fuselage at a point above the ceiling line in the passenger cabin.

Croydon aerodrome

Croydon was London's first real civil airport, opened in 1920. It had searchlights that could be seen for miles, wireless communication between aeroplane and ground, and basic air-traffic control.

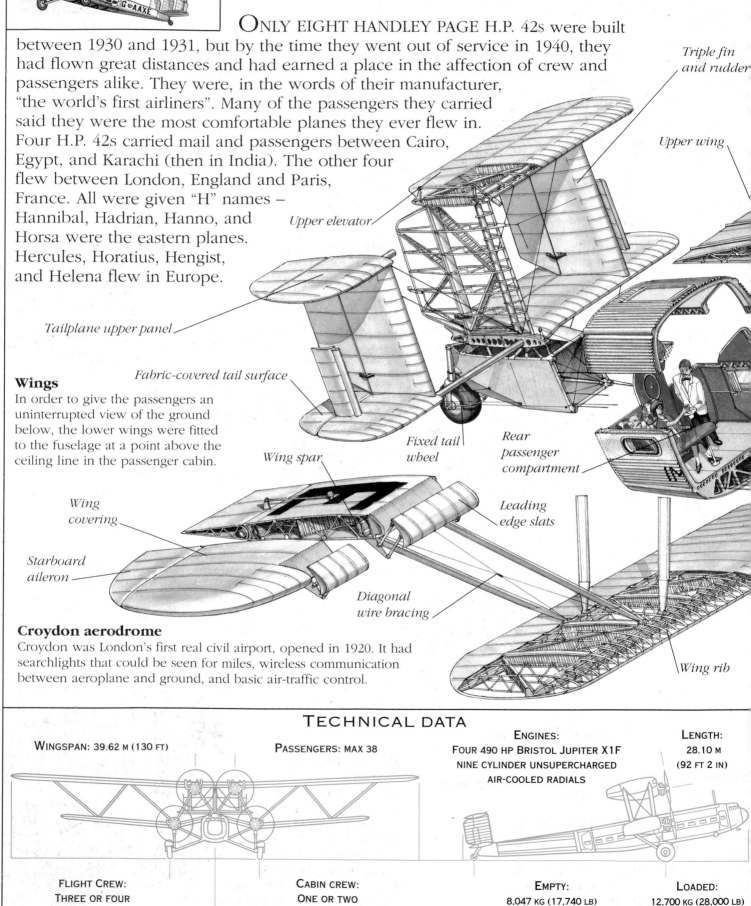

Triple fin and rudder

Upper wing

Upper elevator

Tailplane upper panel

Fabric-covered tail surface

Wing spar

Fixed tail wheel

Rear passenger compartment

Wing covering

Starboard aileron

Leading edge slats

Diagonal wire bracing

Wing rib

TECHNICAL DATA

WINGSPAN: 39.62 M (130 FT)

PASSENGERS: MAX 38

ENGINES:
FOUR 490 HP BRISTOL JUPITER X1F
NINE CYLINDER UNSUPERCHARGED
AIR-COOLED RADIALS

LENGTH:
28.10 M
(92 FT 2 IN)

FLIGHT CREW:
THREE OR FOUR

CABIN CREW:
ONE OR TWO

EMPTY:
8,047 KG (17,740 LB)

LOADED:
12,700 KG (28,000 LB)

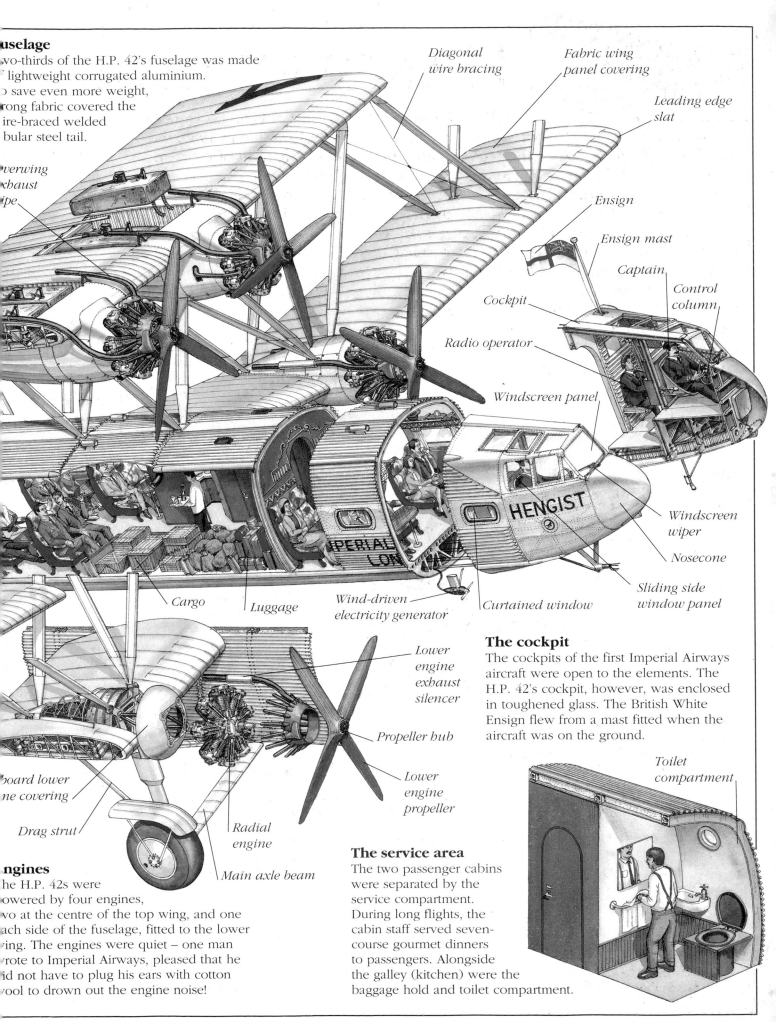

Fuselage
...wo-thirds of the H.P. 42's fuselage was made
...lightweight corrugated aluminium.
...o save even more weight,
...rong fabric covered the
...ire-braced welded
...bular steel tail.

...verwing
...xhaust
...ipe

Diagonal
wire bracing

Fabric wing
panel covering

Leading edge
slat

Ensign

Ensign mast

Captain

Cockpit

Control
column

Radio operator

Windscreen panel

HENGIST

Windscreen
wiper

Nosecone

IMPERIAL
LON...

Sliding side
window panel

Cargo

Luggage

Wind-driven
electricity generator

Curtained window

Lower
engine
exhaust
silencer

Propeller hub

Lower
engine
propeller

...board lower
...ne covering

Drag strut

Radial
engine

Main axle beam

The cockpit
The cockpits of the first Imperial Airways
aircraft were open to the elements. The
H.P. 42's cockpit, however, was enclosed
in toughened glass. The British White
Ensign flew from a mast fitted when the
aircraft was on the ground.

Toilet
compartment

The service area
The two passenger cabins
were separated by the
service compartment.
During long flights, the
cabin staff served seven-
course gourmet dinners
to passengers. Alongside
the galley (kitchen) were the
baggage hold and toilet compartment.

...ngines
...he H.P. 42s were
...owered by four engines,
...vo at the centre of the top wing, and one
...ach side of the fuselage, fitted to the lower
...ving. The engines were quiet – one man
...rote to Imperial Airways, pleased that he
...id not have to plug his ears with cotton
...ool to drown out the engine noise!

BOEING 314

ONLY EIGHT YEARS after the Wright Brothers flew into aviation's history books, another American, Glenn Curtiss, skimmed in by making the first take-off from water, in January 1911. The seaplane had been created. Perhaps the most famous of them was the Boeing 314 which first flew in 1938. In March 1939, *California Clipper* carried passengers from San Francisco to Singapore, and in June that year *Atlantic Clipper* made the first official transatlantic passenger flight. During World War II, the Clippers, known as "flying boats", were used to ferry men and materials all over the world. By the time the War came to an end the 314s had made over 4,10 transoceanic flights. After the war, Clippers could no compete with the new planes being built. The were sold off and later scrapped.

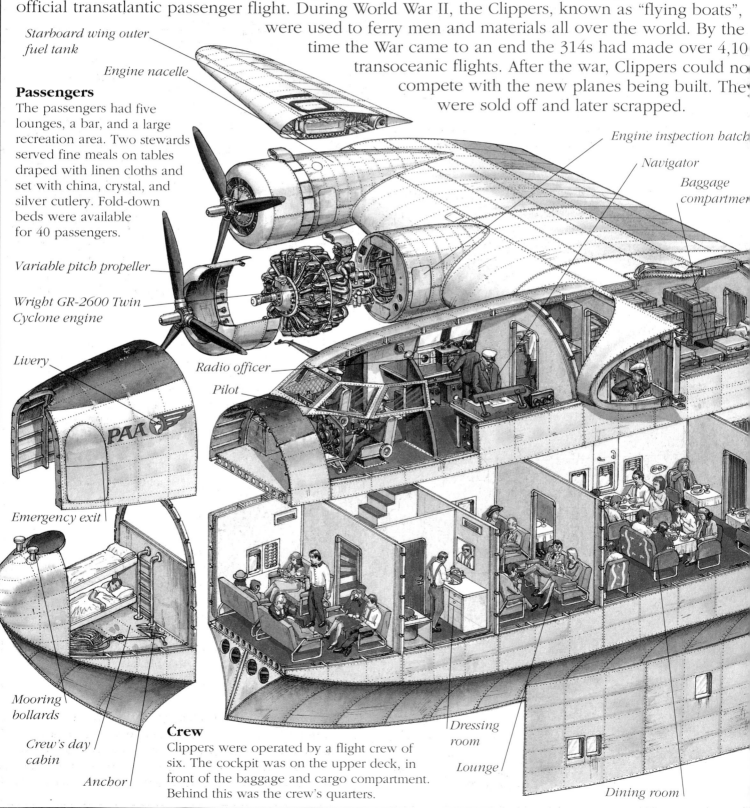

Starboard wing outer fuel tank

Engine nacelle

Passengers
The passengers had five lounges, a bar, and a large recreation area. Two stewards served fine meals on tables draped with linen cloths and set with china, crystal, and silver cutlery. Fold-down beds were available for 40 passengers.

Variable pitch propeller

Wright GR-2600 Twin Cyclone engine

Livery

Radio officer

Pilot

Emergency exit

Engine inspection hatch

Navigator

Baggage compartmen

Mooring bollards

Crew's day cabin

Anchor

Crew
Clippers were operated by a flight crew of six. The cockpit was on the upper deck, in front of the baggage and cargo compartment. Behind this was the crew's quarters.

Dressing room

Lounge

Dining room

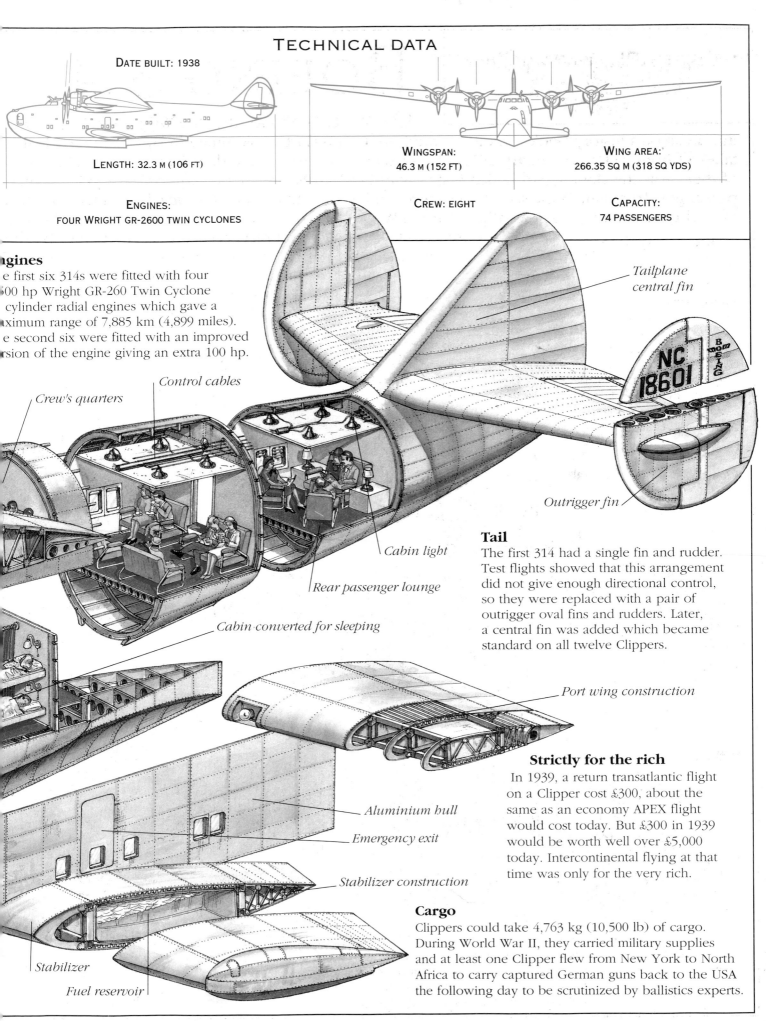

TECHNICAL DATA

DATE BUILT: 1938

LENGTH: 32.3 M (106 FT)

WINGSPAN: 46.3 M (152 FT)

WING AREA: 266.35 SQ M (318 SQ YDS)

ENGINES: FOUR WRIGHT GR-2600 TWIN CYCLONES

CREW: EIGHT

CAPACITY: 74 PASSENGERS

...ngines

...e first six 314s were fitted with four
...00 hp Wright GR-260 Twin Cyclone
...cylinder radial engines which gave a
...ximum range of 7,885 km (4,899 miles).
...e second six were fitted with an improved
...sion of the engine giving an extra 100 hp.

Crew's quarters

Control cables

Tailplane central fin

NC 18601

BOEING

Outrigger fin

Cabin light

Rear passenger lounge

Cabin converted for sleeping

Tail

The first 314 had a single fin and rudder.
Test flights showed that this arrangement
did not give enough directional control,
so they were replaced with a pair of
outrigger oval fins and rudders. Later,
a central fin was added which became
standard on all twelve Clippers.

Port wing construction

Aluminium hull

Emergency exit

Stabilizer construction

Strictly for the rich

In 1939, a return transatlantic flight
on a Clipper cost £300, about the
same as an economy APEX flight
would cost today. But £300 in 1939
would be worth well over £5,000
today. Intercontinental flying at that
time was only for the very rich.

Stabilizer

Fuel reservoir

Cargo

Clippers could take 4,763 kg (10,500 lb) of cargo.
During World War II, they carried military supplies
and at least one Clipper flew from New York to North
Africa to carry captured German guns back to the USA
the following day to be scrutinized by ballistics experts.

Spitfire

THE SPITFIRE CAME INTO BEING because the chief designer of the Supermarine Aviation Works was determined to build an aircraft that would win the famous Schneider Trophy race, an international flying event competed for in the 1920s and 30s. His designs for a racing aeroplane gradually evolved into a fighter, and the prototype (first one) flew in March 1936. The plane was light and easy to fly. It performed so well in trials, exceeding all British requirements for fighter aircraft, that in June of the same year the first production models were ordered.

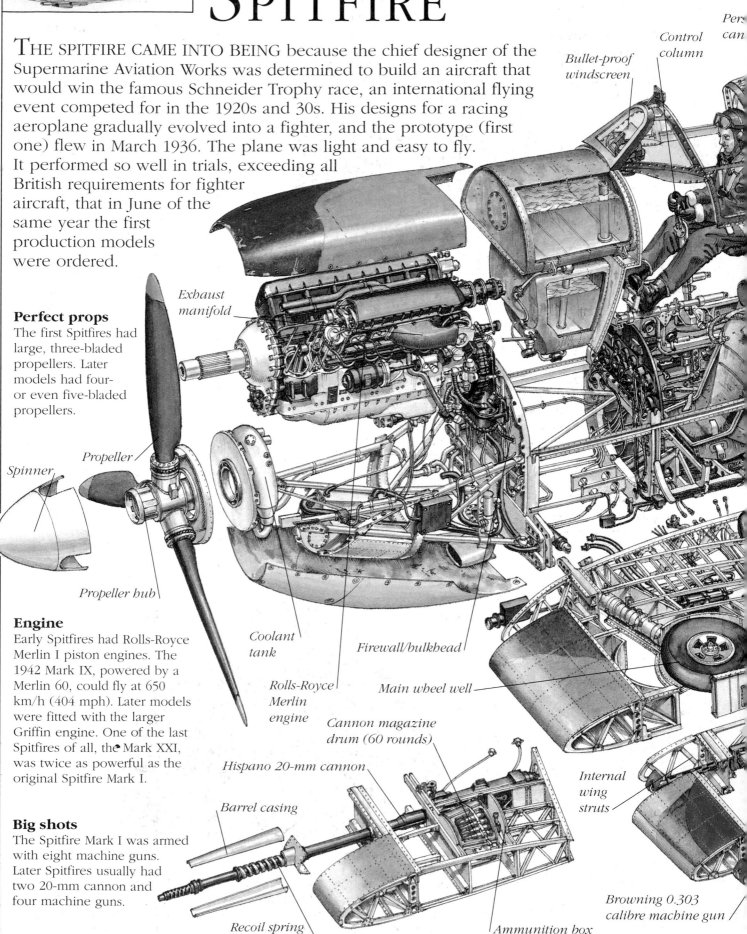

Per...
can...
Control column
Bullet-proof windscreen

Exhaust manifold

Perfect props
The first Spitfires had large, three-bladed propellers. Later models had four- or even five-bladed propellers.

Spinner
Propeller
Propeller hub

Engine
Early Spitfires had Rolls-Royce Merlin I piston engines. The 1942 Mark IX, powered by a Merlin 60, could fly at 650 km/h (404 mph). Later models were fitted with the larger Griffin engine. One of the last Spitfires of all, the Mark XXI, was twice as powerful as the original Spitfire Mark I.

Coolant tank
Firewall/bulkhead
Rolls-Royce Merlin engine
Main wheel well
Cannon magazine drum (60 rounds)
Internal wing struts

Big shots
The Spitfire Mark I was armed with eight machine guns. Later Spitfires usually had two 20-mm cannon and four machine guns.

Hispano 20-mm cannon
Barrel casing
Recoil spring
Ammunition box
Browning 0.303 calibre machine gun

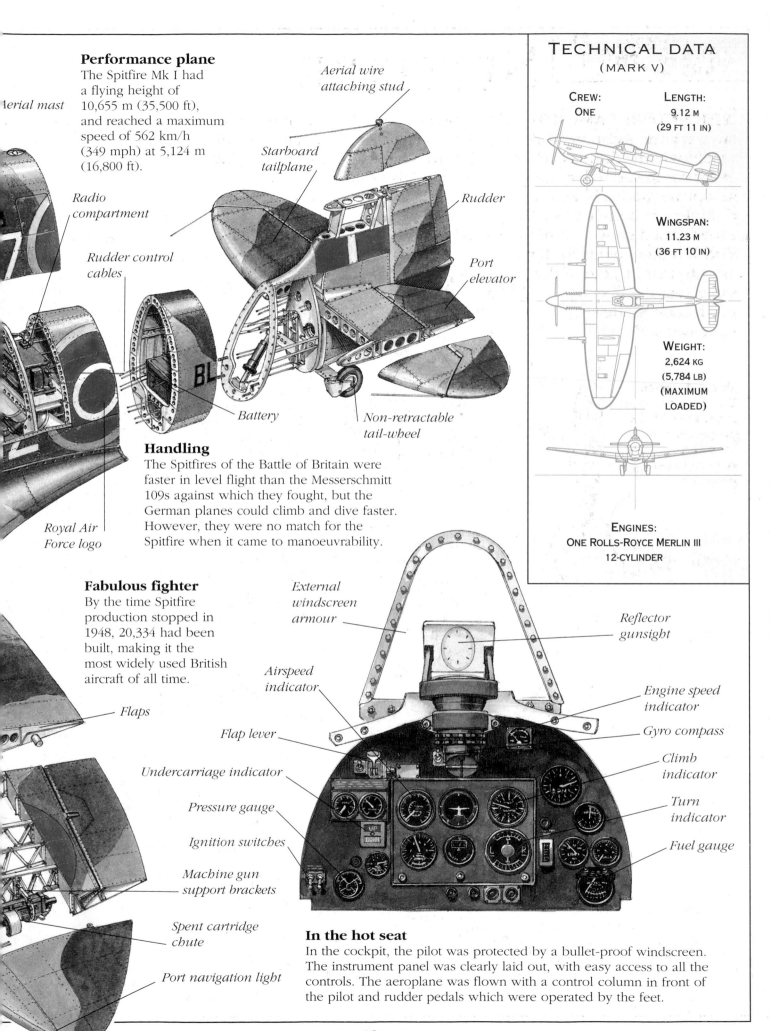

Performance plane
The Spitfire Mk I had a flying height of 10,655 m (35,500 ft), and reached a maximum speed of 562 km/h (349 mph) at 5,124 m (16,800 ft).

Aerial mast

Radio compartment

Rudder control cables

Aerial wire attaching stud

Starboard tailplane

Rudder

Port elevator

Battery

Non-retractable tail-wheel

Royal Air Force logo

Handling
The Spitfires of the Battle of Britain were faster in level flight than the Messerschmitt 109s against which they fought, but the German planes could climb and dive faster. However, they were no match for the Spitfire when it came to manoeuvrability.

Fabulous fighter
By the time Spitfire production stopped in 1948, 20,334 had been built, making it the most widely used British aircraft of all time.

Flaps

Flap lever

Undercarriage indicator

Pressure gauge

Ignition switches

Machine gun support brackets

Spent cartridge chute

Port navigation light

External windscreen armour

Airspeed indicator

Reflector gunsight

Engine speed indicator

Gyro compass

Climb indicator

Turn indicator

Fuel gauge

In the hot seat
In the cockpit, the pilot was protected by a bullet-proof windscreen. The instrument panel was clearly laid out, with easy access to all the controls. The aeroplane was flown with a control column in front of the pilot and rudder pedals which were operated by the feet.

TECHNICAL DATA
(MARK V)

CREW:
ONE

LENGTH:
9.12 M
(29 FT 11 IN)

WINGSPAN:
11.23 M
(36 FT 10 IN)

WEIGHT:
2,624 KG
(5,784 LB)
(MAXIMUM LOADED)

ENGINES:
ONE ROLLS-ROYCE MERLIN III
12-CYLINDER

FLYING FORTRESS

IMAGINE A HUGE FORTRESS lifting off the ground and flying through the air. Bristling with guns and packed with bombs, it would be a sight to strike fear into any enemy. The US B-17 bomber was just such a sight. Mainstay of bombing operations in Europe during World War II, it was also widely used in the Pacific, the Middle East, and the Far East. The B-17 made its first appearance in 1935 as Boeing's prototype Model 299. It was given its official designation, B-17, after its trials for the US Army. The B-17G, which was introduced in 1943, was armed with twin machine guns in the chin, dorsal, ventral, and tail gun turrets plus two in the nose, one in the radio compartment, and one in each waist position.

Bombs
The B-17s normally carried 2,724 kg (6,000 lb) of bombs, but they could carry more than double that. The bombs were controlled by the bombardier who sat in the plane's nose.

Radio operator's compartment

Windscreen

Good-luck mascot painting

Bomb-bay bulkhead

Dorsal gun turret

Bomb store

Up front
The pilot and co-pilot sat alongside each other in the cramped cockpit. The glass surrounding it was tough but not bullet-proof.

Co-pilot

Navigator's compartment

Bombardier

Pilot

Navigator

Norden bombsight

Nose machine guns

Port main wheel

Engines
The B-17G was powered by four Wright Cyclone engines. These gave it a maximum speed of 462 km/h (287 mph). Even early in its career, the B-17 made long-distance flights, including one from Miami to Buenos Aires – a distance of 8,465 km (5,260 miles).

Optically flat bomb-aiming panel

Plexiglass frameless nose cone

Bomb

Detonator

High explosive

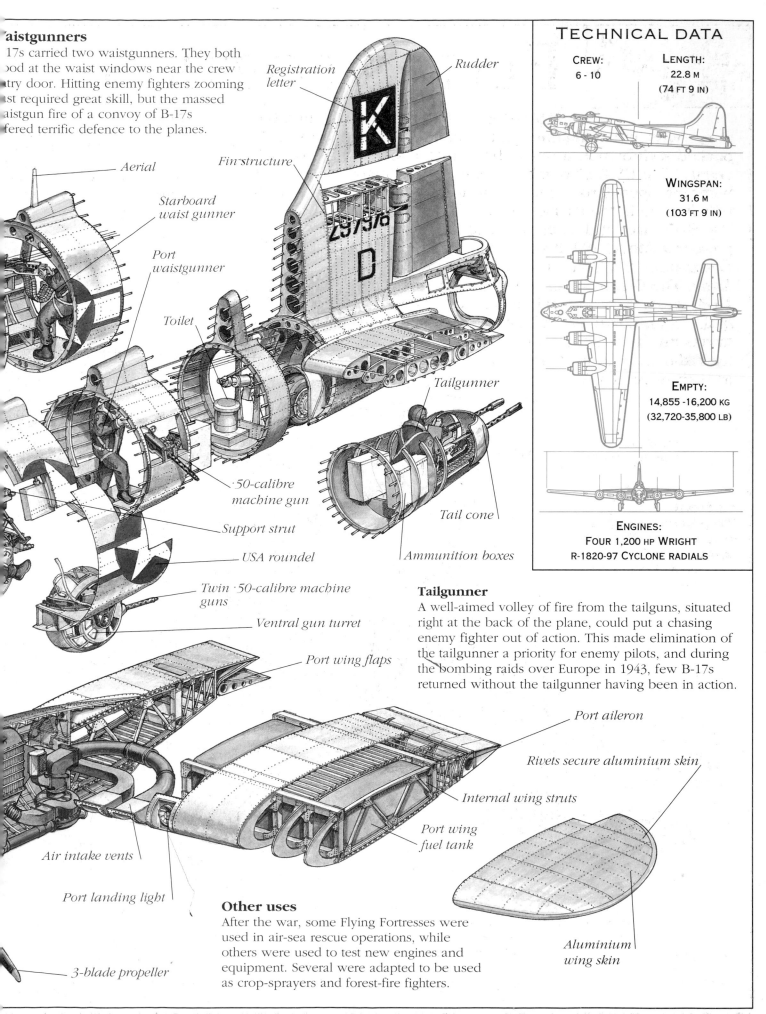

Waistgunners

17s carried two waistgunners. They both
od at the waist windows near the crew
try door. Hitting enemy fighters zooming
st required great skill, but the massed
aistgun fire of a convoy of B-17s
fered terrific defence to the planes.

Rudder

Registration
letter

Fin structure

Aerial

Starboard
waist gunner

Port
waistgunner

Toilet

Tailgunner

·50-calibre
machine gun

Support strut

USA roundel

Tail cone

Ammunition boxes

Twin ·50-calibre machine
guns

Ventral gun turret

Port wing flaps

TECHNICAL DATA

CREW:	LENGTH:
6 - 10	22.8 M (74 FT 9 IN)

WINGSPAN:
31.6 M
(103 FT 9 IN)

EMPTY:
14,855 -16,200 KG
(32,720-35,800 LB)

ENGINES:
FOUR 1,200 HP WRIGHT
R-1820-97 CYCLONE RADIALS

Tailgunner

A well-aimed volley of fire from the tailguns, situated
right at the back of the plane, could put a chasing
enemy fighter out of action. This made elimination of
the tailgunner a priority for enemy pilots, and during
the bombing raids over Europe in 1943, few B-17s
returned without the tailgunner having been in action.

Port aileron

Rivets secure aluminium skin

Internal wing struts

Port wing
fuel tank

Air intake vents

Port landing light

Other uses

After the war, some Flying Fortresses were
used in air-sea rescue operations, while
others were used to test new engines and
equipment. Several were adapted to be used
as crop-sprayers and forest-fire fighters.

3-blade propeller

Aluminium
wing skin

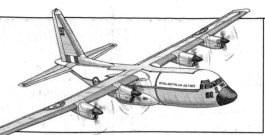

HERCULES

"YOU BUILD TOUGH AIRPLANES!" That's what the Governor of Georgia, USA, said in 1954 after he had "launched" the first production C-130 Hercules by breaking a bottle of water over its nose. It had taken four attempts before the glass shattered. The Hercules is indeed tough. More than 1,700 have been produced in 40 or so versions. They still roll off the production lines at the rate of about three a month. They are flown by over 50 of the world's air forces and have proved their ruggedness over and over again in war and in peacetime. The C-130 can land on sand, snow, rough terrain, and on aircraft carriers. There has even been a Hercules aerobatic team!

The cockpit

The pilot and co-pilot sit alongside each other at the front of the cockpit which is extremely spacious. Behind them is the navigation station and the systems engineer's seat. The cockpit is equipped with rest bunks where the crew take it in turns to sleep during long flights.

Radar

The C-130, like all modern aircraft, is equipped with radar. When the radio waves sent out by the transmitter hit an object they are reflected back to the radar station. The signal passes through a cathode ray tube on which an image of what the radio beam has hit appears. Aircraft use radar to detect other aircraft, locate targets, and warn of approaching bad weather.

Crew rest bunks

Forward escape hatch

Windscreen panel

ROYAL AUS

Navigator

Co-pilot

Instrument panel

Pilot

Rudder pedal

Weather radar scanner

Radome

Radome mounting framework

Front bulkhead

Twin nosewheel

Crew entry door

Fligh deck acce lada

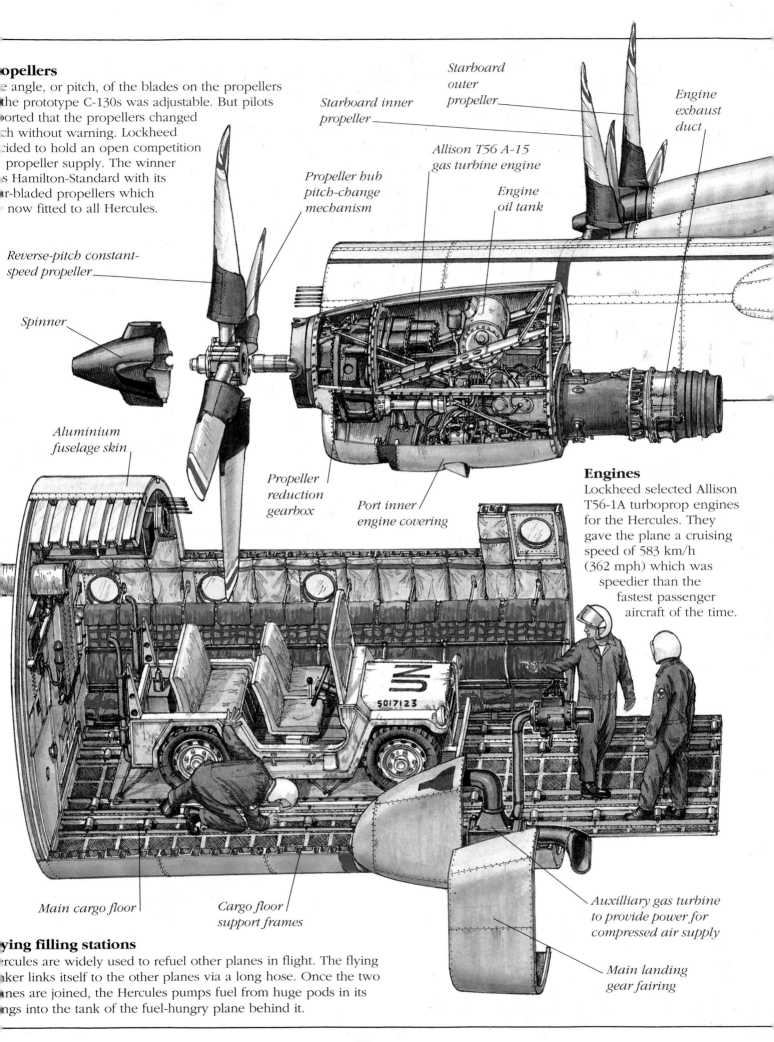

...opellers

...e angle, or pitch, of the blades on the propellers
...the prototype C-130s was adjustable. But pilots
...orted that the propellers changed
...ch without warning. Lockheed
...cided to hold an open competition
... propeller supply. The winner
...s Hamilton-Standard with its
...r-bladed propellers which
... now fitted to all Hercules.

**Reverse-pitch constant-
speed propeller**

Spinner

**Aluminium
fuselage skin**

**Propeller hub
pitch-change
mechanism**

**Starboard inner
propeller**

**Starboard
outer
propeller**

**Allison T56 A-15
gas turbine engine**

**Engine
oil tank**

**Engine
exhaust
duct**

**Propeller
reduction
gearbox**

**Port inner
engine covering**

Engines
Lockheed selected Allison
T56-1A turboprop engines
for the Hercules. They
gave the plane a cruising
speed of 583 km/h
(362 mph) which was
speedier than the
fastest passenger
aircraft of the time.

Main cargo floor

**Cargo floor
support frames**

**Auxilliary gas turbine
to provide power for
compressed air supply**

**Main landing
gear fairing**

...ying filling stations
...rcules are widely used to refuel other planes in flight. The flying
...ker links itself to the other planes via a long hose. Once the two
...nes are joined, the Hercules pumps fuel from huge pods in its
...ngs into the tank of the fuel-hungry plane behind it.

Starboard aileron

Fuel filler cap

In the Arctic
In 1965 Alaska Airways leased a Hercules from Lockheed. Within 20 days had hauled oil-drilling equipment betwe Fairbanks and a site near the Arctic Oce Eventually five more "Herks" were lease and they played a vital part in the oil rus that opened up the region in the 1970s.

Escape hatch

Toilet compartm curtain

Wing centre section construction

Fuel tank

Port paratro door

To

Cargo loading ramp

Shock absorber

Axle bearing

Tandem twin mainwheel

Main landing gear outer door

Capacity
Different models of the Hercules can carry differing amounts of cargo and troops. The C-130H-30, which is i wide use around the world, can carry seven cargo pallet four Land-rovers, and four trailers. It can take up to 128 paratroopers – but only 92 if they are fully armed.

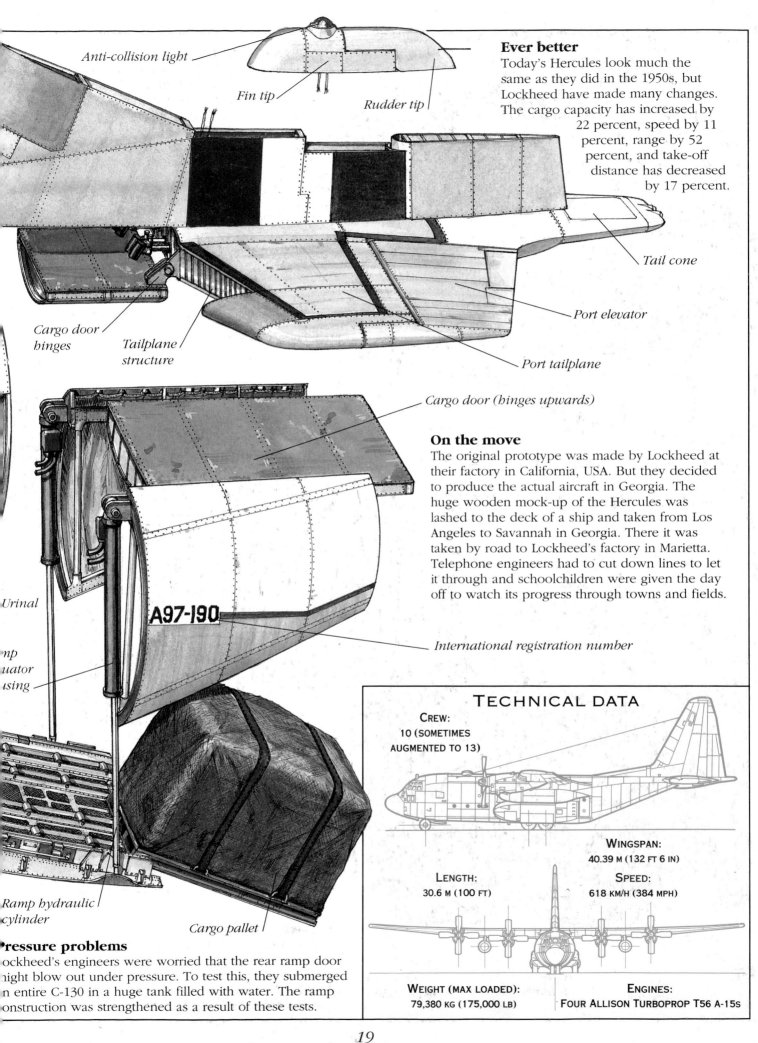

Anti-collision light

Fin tip

Rudder tip

Ever better

Today's Hercules look much the same as they did in the 1950s, but Lockheed have made many changes. The cargo capacity has increased by 22 percent, speed by 11 percent, range by 52 percent, and take-off distance has decreased by 17 percent.

Tail cone

Cargo door hinges

Tailplane structure

Port elevator

Port tailplane

Cargo door (hinges upwards)

On the move

The original prototype was made by Lockheed at their factory in California, USA. But they decided to produce the actual aircraft in Georgia. The huge wooden mock-up of the Hercules was lashed to the deck of a ship and taken from Los Angeles to Savannah in Georgia. There it was taken by road to Lockheed's factory in Marietta. Telephone engineers had to cut down lines to let it through and schoolchildren were given the day off to watch its progress through towns and fields.

Urinal

np uator using

A97-190

International registration number

Ramp hydraulic cylinder

Cargo pallet

Pressure problems

ockheed's engineers were worried that the rear ramp door ight blow out under pressure. To test this, they submerged n entire C-130 in a huge tank filled with water. The ramp onstruction was strengthened as a result of these tests.

TECHNICAL DATA

CREW:
10 (SOMETIMES AUGMENTED TO 13)

WINGSPAN:
40.39 M (132 FT 6 IN)

LENGTH:
30.6 M (100 FT)

SPEED:
618 KM/H (384 MPH)

WEIGHT (MAX LOADED):
79,380 KG (175,000 LB)

ENGINES:
FOUR ALLISON TURBOPROP T56 A-15S

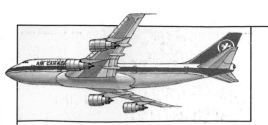

BOEING 747

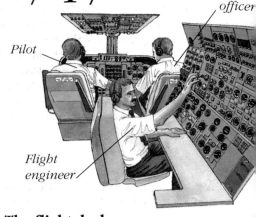

IN 1960, THE WORLD'S
airlines carried more than 106 million passengers. By 1966
this had mushroomed to 200 million. The volume of cargo
being carried by air also soared. As more and more
aeroplanes took to the skies, airports became more and
more crowded, and so, to absorb this dramatic increase,
manufacturers decided to try to make larger aircraft. The first
of the wide-bodied aeroplanes was Boeing's 747. It first flew
on 9 February 1969. Less than a year later, it entered service
on the transatlantic route with Pan American airlines, carrying
more than 350 passengers from New York to London. With
one bold step, Boeing had doubled the capacity, power,
and weight of transport aircraft. No wonder this
mammoth machine was called "Jumbo". The
name stuck and the 747 and its
successors have all been
called "Jumbo Jets".

The flight deck
Most 747s are flown by a three-person crew
pilot, first officer, and flight engineer. The
pilot and first officer sit alongside each othe
with the flight engineer behind. The 747-40
introduced in 1988 has a two-crew flight de

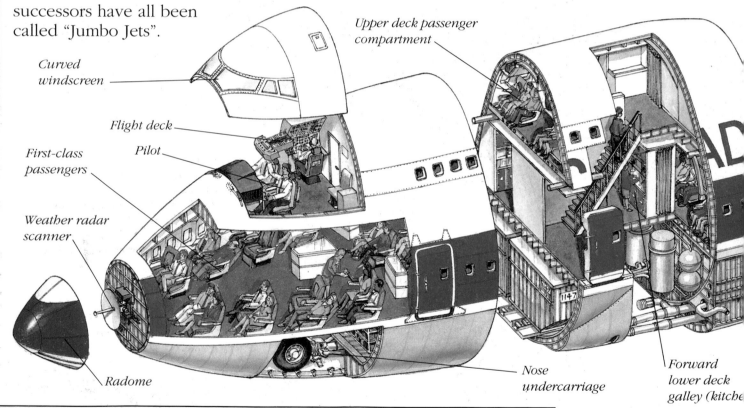

Curved
windscreen

Flight deck

First-class
passengers

Pilot

Weather radar
scanner

Radome

Upper deck passenger
compartment

Nose
undercarriage

Forward
lower deck
galley (kitche

TECHNICAL DATA

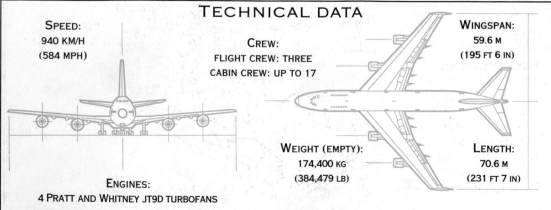

SPEED:
940 KM/H
(584 MPH)

CREW:
FLIGHT CREW: THREE
CABIN CREW: UP TO 17

WINGSPAN:
59.6 M
(195 FT 6 IN)

WEIGHT (EMPTY):
174,400 KG
(384,479 LB)

LENGTH:
70.6 M
(231 FT 7 IN)

ENGINES:
4 PRATT AND WHITNEY JT9D TURBOFANS

747 variations
747 variations include the
747SP (Special Purpose) whi
is 15 m (49 ft) shorter than t
standard 747, but which has
higher tail fin. It flies faster a
farther than any other subso
aircraft. On a delivery flight
March 1976, one was flown
non-stop from Seattle, USA,
to Cape Town, South Africa.

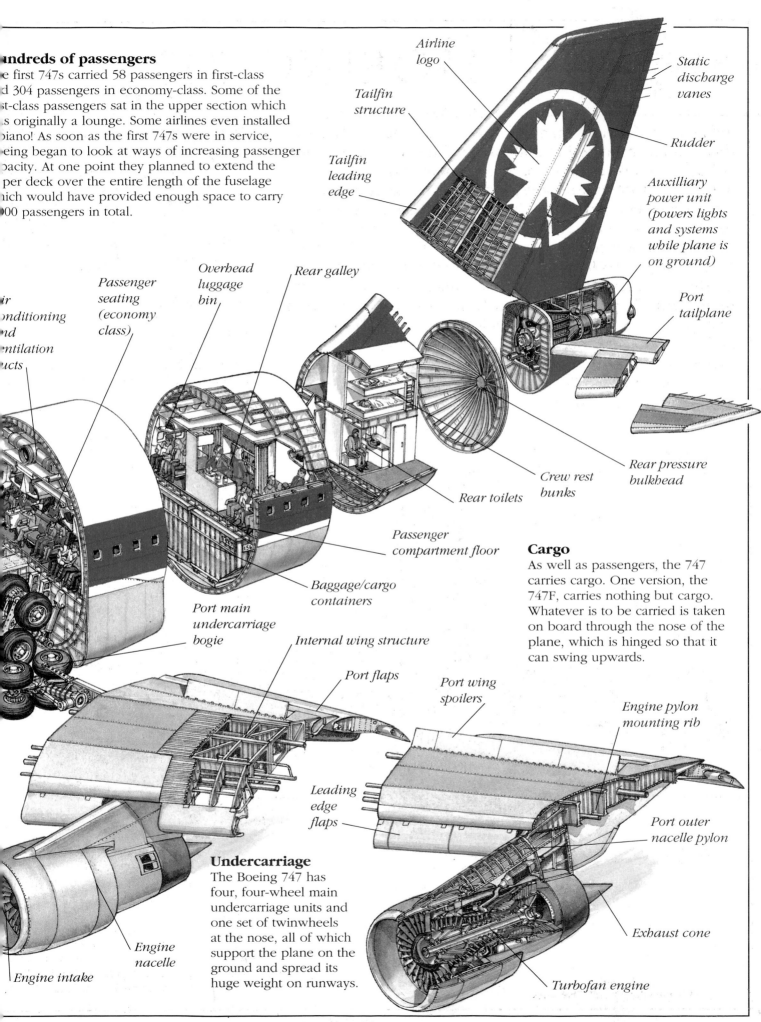

undreds of passengers

e first 747s carried 58 passengers in first-class
d 304 passengers in economy-class. Some of the
st-class passengers sat in the upper section which
s originally a lounge. Some airlines even installed
iano! As soon as the first 747s were in service,
eing began to look at ways of increasing passenger
acity. At one point they planned to extend the
per deck over the entire length of the fuselage
ich would have provided enough space to carry
00 passengers in total.

Airline logo

Static discharge vanes

Tailfin structure

Rudder

Tailfin leading edge

Auxilliary power unit (powers lights and systems while plane is on ground)

Port tailplane

Overhead luggage bin

Rear galley

Passenger seating (economy class)

ir nditioning nd ntilation ucts

Crew rest bunks

Rear pressure bulkhead

Rear toilets

Passenger compartment floor

Cargo

As well as passengers, the 747 carries cargo. One version, the 747F, carries nothing but cargo. Whatever is to be carried is taken on board through the nose of the plane, which is hinged so that it can swing upwards.

Baggage/cargo containers

Port main undercarriage bogie

Internal wing structure

Port flaps

Port wing spoilers

Engine pylon mounting rib

Leading edge flaps

Port outer nacelle pylon

Undercarriage

The Boeing 747 has four, four-wheel main undercarriage units and one set of twinwheels at the nose, all of which support the plane on the ground and spread its huge weight on runways.

Engine nacelle

Engine intake

Exhaust cone

Turbofan engine

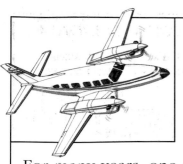

PIPER CHIEFTAIN

LIGHT AIRCRAFT ARE USED FOR CROP-SPRAYING, air-sea rescue, and fire-fighting. They also carry small numbers of passengers from place to place. They can land in places unsuitable for large aircraft. For many years, one of the leading light aircraft manufacturers has been the Piper Corporation of the USA. They have produced an enormous variety of small aeroplanes ranging from single-seaters that can fly so low that the pilots sometimes feel they can lean out of the cockpit and touch the treetops, to sophisticated jets that carry up to ten people in luxury. Piper aircraft, including the Chieftain PA-31, are popular with airlines around the world. In fact they are so successful that Piper set up its own airline division in 1981.

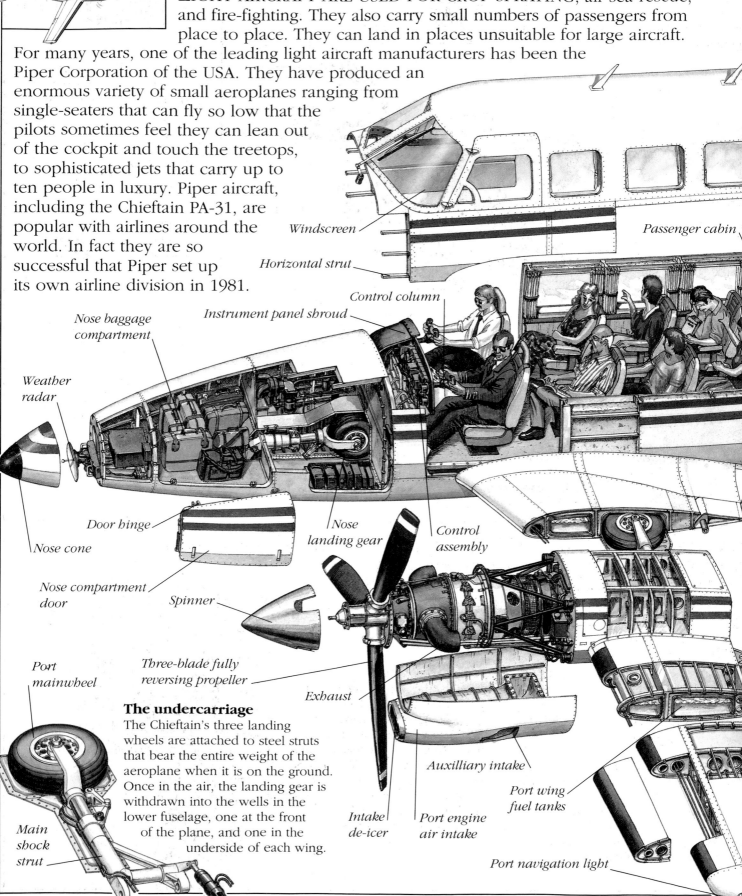

Windscreen

Passenger cabin

Horizontal strut

Control column

Instrument panel shroud

Nose baggage compartment

Weather radar

Nose landing gear

Control assembly

Door hinge

Nose cone

Nose compartment door

Spinner

Port mainwheel

Three-blade fully reversing propeller

Exhaust

The undercarriage
The Chieftain's three landing wheels are attached to steel struts that bear the entire weight of the aeroplane when it is on the ground. Once in the air, the landing gear is withdrawn into the wells in the lower fuselage, one at the front of the plane, and one in the underside of each wing.

Auxilliary intake

Intake de-icer

Port engine air intake

Port wing fuel tanks

Main shock strut

Port navigation light

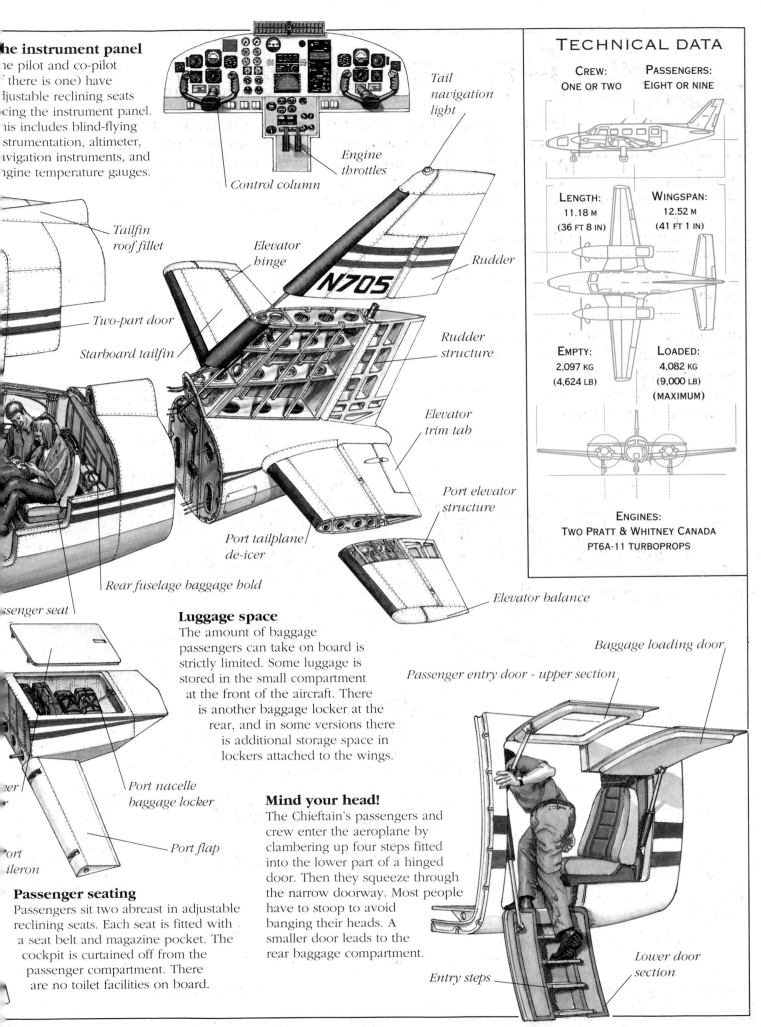

The instrument panel

The pilot and co-pilot (if there is one) have adjustable reclining seats facing the instrument panel. This includes blind-flying instrumentation, altimeter, navigation instruments, and engine temperature gauges.

Control column

Engine throttles

Tail navigation light

Tailfin roof fillet

Elevator hinge

Two-part door

Starboard tailfin

Rudder

Rudder structure

Elevator trim tab

Elevator balance

Port elevator structure

Port tailplane de-icer

Rear fuselage baggage hold

Passenger seat

Port nacelle baggage locker

Port flap

Port aileron

TECHNICAL DATA

CREW: ONE OR TWO

PASSENGERS: EIGHT OR NINE

LENGTH: 11.18 M (36 FT 8 IN)

WINGSPAN: 12.52 M (41 FT 1 IN)

EMPTY: 2,097 KG (4,624 LB)

LOADED: 4,082 KG (9,000 LB) (MAXIMUM)

ENGINES: TWO PRATT & WHITNEY CANADA PT6A-11 TURBOPROPS

Luggage space

The amount of baggage passengers can take on board is strictly limited. Some luggage is stored in the small compartment at the front of the aircraft. There is another baggage locker at the rear, and in some versions there is additional storage space in lockers attached to the wings.

Passenger seating

Passengers sit two abreast in adjustable reclining seats. Each seat is fitted with a seat belt and magazine pocket. The cockpit is curtained off from the passenger compartment. There are no toilet facilities on board.

Mind your head!

The Chieftain's passengers and crew enter the aeroplane by clambering up four steps fitted into the lower part of a hinged door. Then they squeeze through the narrow doorway. Most people have to stoop to avoid banging their heads. A smaller door leads to the rear baggage compartment.

Baggage loading door

Passenger entry door - upper section

Lower door section

Entry steps

23

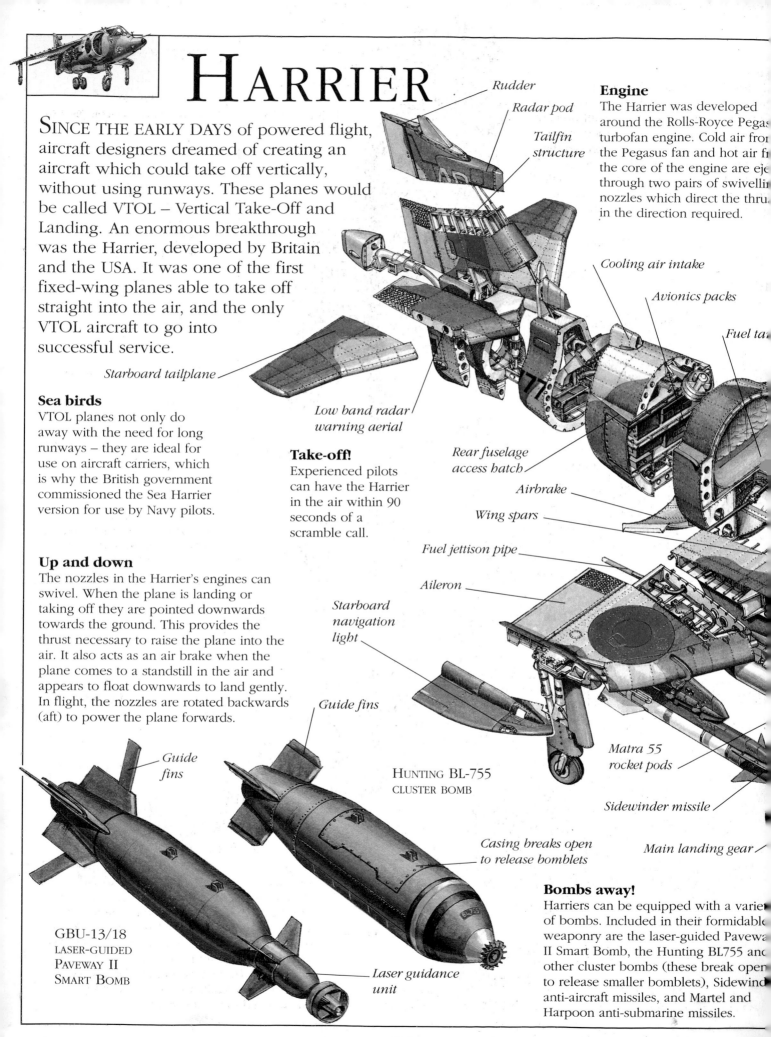

HARRIER

SINCE THE EARLY DAYS of powered flight, aircraft designers dreamed of creating an aircraft which could take off vertically, without using runways. These planes would be called VTOL – Vertical Take-Off and Landing. An enormous breakthrough was the Harrier, developed by Britain and the USA. It was one of the first fixed-wing planes able to take off straight into the air, and the only VTOL aircraft to go into successful service.

Starboard tailplane

Sea birds

VTOL planes not only do away with the need for long runways – they are ideal for use on aircraft carriers, which is why the British government commissioned the Sea Harrier version for use by Navy pilots.

Up and down

The nozzles in the Harrier's engines can swivel. When the plane is landing or taking off they are pointed downwards towards the ground. This provides the thrust necessary to raise the plane into the air. It also acts as an air brake when the plane comes to a standstill in the air and appears to float downwards to land gently. In flight, the nozzles are rotated backwards (aft) to power the plane forwards.

Guide fins

GBU-13/18
LASER-GUIDED
PAVEWAY II
SMART BOMB

Laser guidance unit

Rudder

Radar pod

Tailfin structure

Low band radar warning aerial

Take-off!

Experienced pilots can have the Harrier in the air within 90 seconds of a scramble call.

Starboard navigation light

Guide fins

HUNTING BL-755
CLUSTER BOMB

Casing breaks open to release bomblets

Engine

The Harrier was developed around the Rolls-Royce Pegas turbofan engine. Cold air from the Pegasus fan and hot air fr the core of the engine are eje through two pairs of swivellin nozzles which direct the thru in the direction required.

Cooling air intake

Avionics packs

Fuel ta

Rear fuselage access hatch

Airbrake

Wing spars

Fuel jettison pipe

Aileron

Matra 55 rocket pods

Sidewinder missile

Main landing gear

Bombs away!

Harriers can be equipped with a varie of bombs. Included in their formidable weaponry are the laser-guided Pavewa II Smart Bomb, the Hunting BL755 and other cluster bombs (these break open to release smaller bomblets), Sidewind anti-aircraft missiles, and Martel and Harpoon anti-submarine missiles.

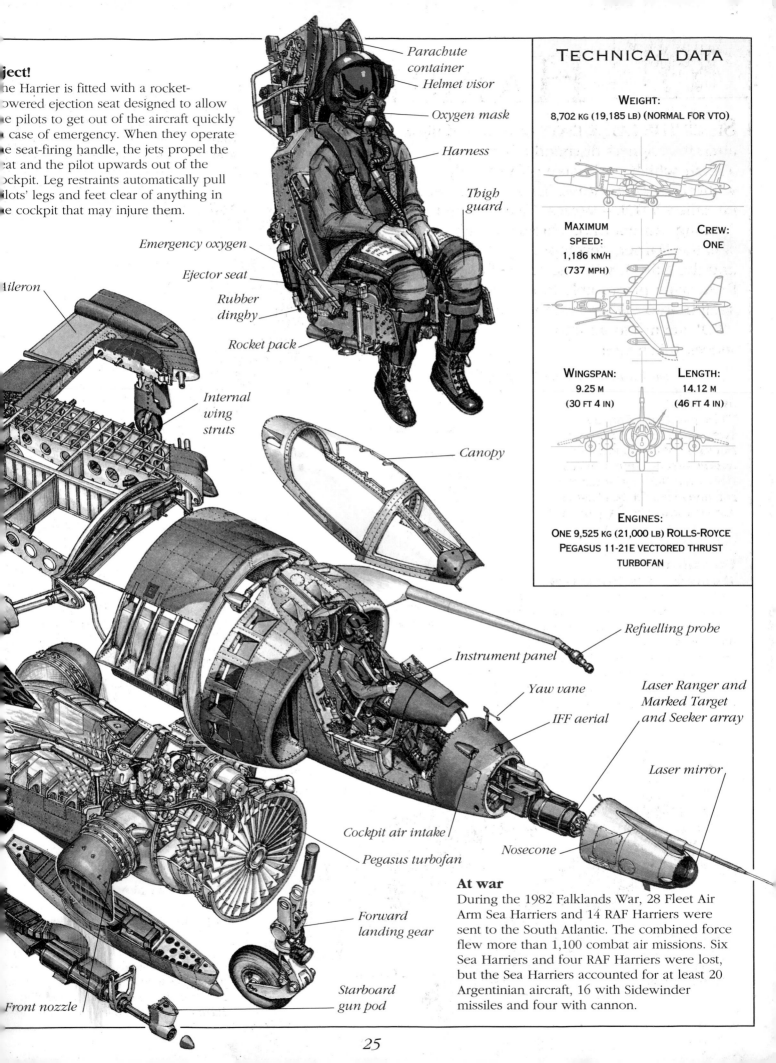

...ject!

...he Harrier is fitted with a rocket-
...owered ejection seat designed to allow
...e pilots to get out of the aircraft quickly
... case of emergency. When they operate
...e seat-firing handle, the jets propel the
...at and the pilot upwards out of the
...ockpit. Leg restraints automatically pull
...lots' legs and feet clear of anything in
...e cockpit that may injure them.

Parachute
container

Helmet visor

Oxygen mask

Harness

Thigh
guard

Emergency oxygen

Ejector seat

Rubber
dingby

Rocket pack

Aileron

Internal
wing
struts

Canopy

Refuelling probe

Instrument panel

Yaw vane

Laser Ranger and
Marked Target
and Seeker array

IFF aerial

Laser mirror

Cockpit air intake

Nosecone

Pegasus turbofan

Forward
landing gear

Front nozzle

Starboard
gun pod

At war

During the 1982 Falklands War, 28 Fleet Air
Arm Sea Harriers and 14 RAF Harriers were
sent to the South Atlantic. The combined force
flew more than 1,100 combat air missions. Six
Sea Harriers and four RAF Harriers were lost,
but the Sea Harriers accounted for at least 20
Argentinian aircraft, 16 with Sidewinder
missiles and four with cannon.

CONCORDE

IMAGINE HAVING BREAKFAST IN LONDON, going to the airport and boarding a plane that whisks you to New York in time for – breakfast! Thanks to the time difference between the two cities, you could do just that if you flew on Concorde. Concorde is the only supersonic passenger aircraft in commercial service. It is very expensive to operate and passengers have to pay much more to fly on it than they do on airliners that fly at less than the speed of sound. First-time Concorde passengers are sometimes surprised at how cramped the cabin is. Business travellers and other regular users find that the service Concorde offers is indispensable, but when it first flew there were complaints about the noise it made. Everyone agrees on one thing, though. Concorde is one of the most beautiful aircraft ever to grace the skies.

Controls

The way that people use machines is part of a science called ergonomics, and experts in this field were deeply involved in helping to plan Concorde's flight deck. It was designed so that everything is in the most convenient position. The captain and the co-pilot sit side by side facing the control panel. The flight engineer sits behind them. The nose of Concorde lowers at take-off and landing to improve crew visibility.

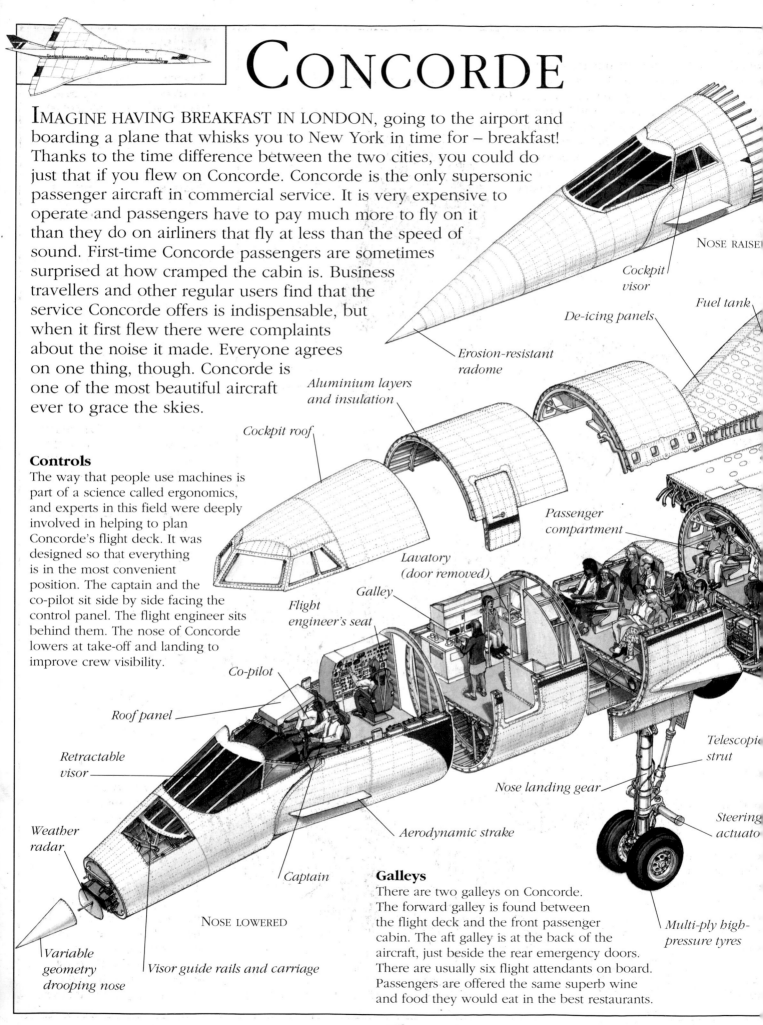

NOSE RAISED

Cockpit visor

Fuel tank

De-icing panels

Erosion-resistant radome

Aluminium layers and insulation

Cockpit roof

Passenger compartment

Lavatory (door removed)

Galley

Flight engineer's seat

Co-pilot

Roof panel

Retractable visor

Telescopic strut

Nose landing gear

Steering actuator

Weather radar

Aerodynamic strake

Multi-ply high-pressure tyres

Captain

NOSE LOWERED

Variable geometry drooping nose

Visor guide rails and carriage

Galleys

There are two galleys on Concorde. The forward galley is found between the flight deck and the front passenger cabin. The aft galley is at the back of the aircraft, just beside the rear emergency doors. There are usually six flight attendants on board. Passengers are offered the same superb wine and food they would eat in the best restaurants.

eed

ncorde travels at more than twice Mach 1 (the
ne for the speed of sound). This means it is
ersonic. When an aeroplane travels faster than
ch 1, it goes "through the sound barrier", and
kes a very loud, echoing boom. The main
ncorde operators ordered their crews to fly
wer than Mach 1 (at subsonic speed) until the
craft was flying over the sea, or when it was
ng too high for the sound to affect anyone.

nter-elevon
lexible joint

*Tailfin
structure*

*Combined secondary
nozzle/reverse buckets*

VHF omni-range aerial

Upper rudder

Livery

Tail cone

*Rear baggage
compartment*

*Emergency
exit*

*Internal
wing
structure*

Shock absorber

t main landing gear

wheel bogie

nding
ar

ncorde
es off and lands
ten multi-ply high-
ssure tyres. There
four on each main
ding bogie, and
o on the nose
ding gear.

ake
ct

Mainwheel leg

Bogie beam

*Rolls-Royce
engine*

Primary heat exchanger

*Port elevon
(combined
elevator and
aileron)*

Engines

The four Rolls-Royce
turbojet engines are fitted
two in each wing. Each one
has a silencer to cut down
engine noise. The engines
are also fitted with thrust
reversers which help the
plane to stop when it lands.

AIRCRAFT TIMELINE

In 1900, POWERED FLIGHT was the fantasy of a few. Today it is a reality to virtually anyone. In 1903, Orville Wright made the first flight in a heavier-than-air, powered machine. Today his plane would fit into a small corner of a C-130 Hercules. Here are some milestones in the story of flight.

1903 WRIGHT FLYER

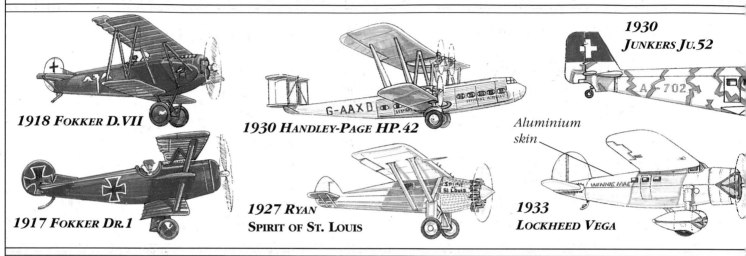

1918 FOKKER D.VII

1917 FOKKER DR.1

1930 HANDLEY-PAGE HP.42

1927 RYAN SPIRIT OF ST. LOUIS

1930 JUNKERS JU.52

Aluminium skin

1933 LOCKHEED VEGA

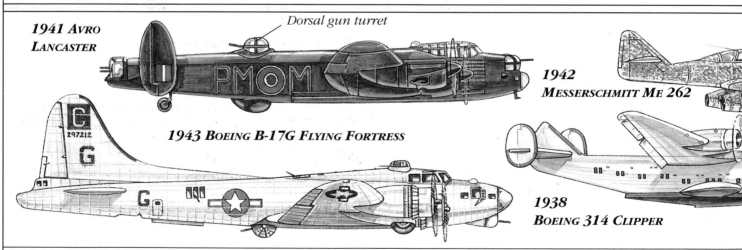

1941 AVRO LANCASTER

Dorsal gun turret

1943 BOEING B-17G FLYING FORTRESS

1942 MESSERSCHMITT ME 262

1938 BOEING 314 CLIPPER

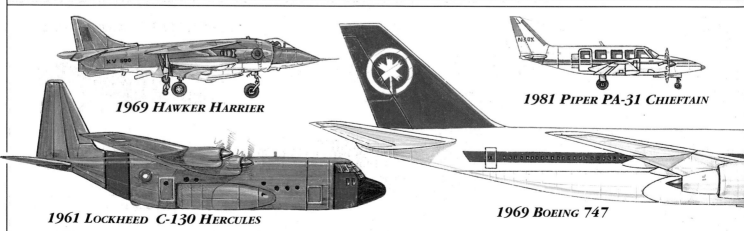

1969 HAWKER HARRIER

1981 PIPER PA-31 CHIEFTAIN

1961 LOCKHEED C-130 HERCULES

1969 BOEING 747

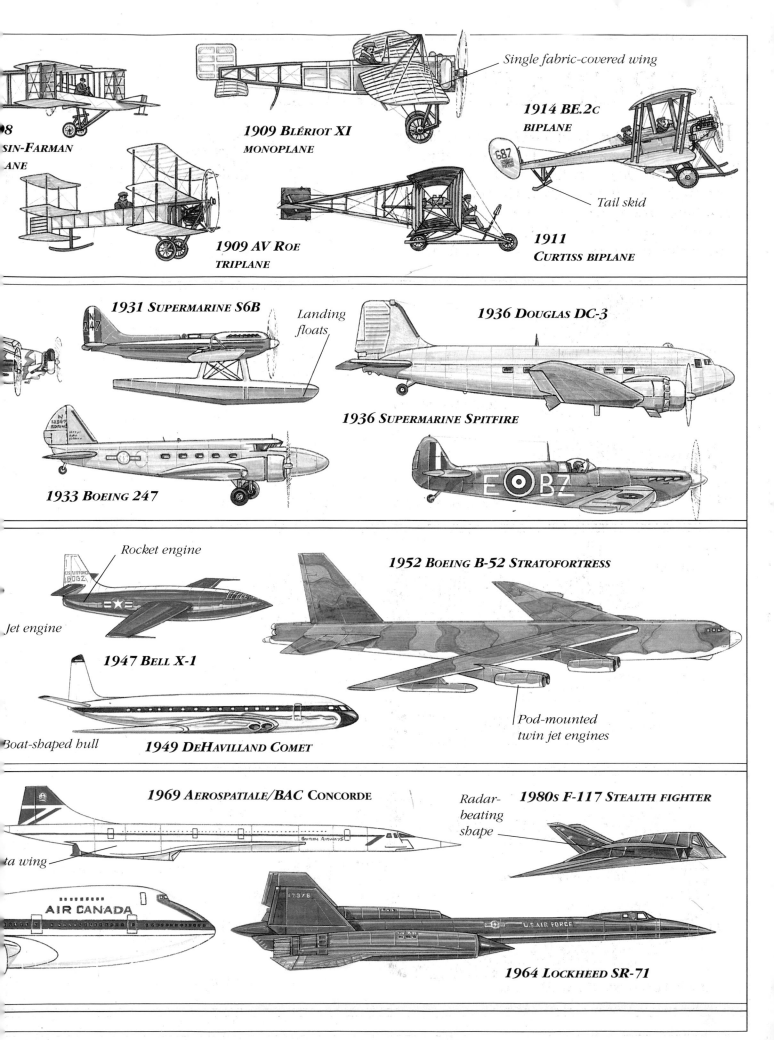

8
SIN-FARMAN
ANE

1909 BLÉRIOT XI
MONOPLANE

Single fabric-covered wing

1914 BE.2c
BIPLANE

Tail skid

1909 AV ROE
TRIPLANE

1911
CURTISS BIPLANE

1931 SUPERMARINE S6B

Landing floats

1936 DOUGLAS DC-3

1936 SUPERMARINE SPITFIRE

1933 BOEING 247

Rocket engine

1952 BOEING B-52 STRATOFORTRESS

Jet engine

1947 BELL X-1

Boat-shaped hull

1949 DEHAVILLAND COMET

Pod-mounted twin jet engines

1969 AEROSPATIALE/BAC CONCORDE

Radar-beating shape

1980s F-117 STEALTH FIGHTER

ta wing

AIR CANADA

1964 LOCKHEED SR-71

GLOSSARY

Aerofoil
A shaped structure that causes lift when propelled through the air. A wing, propeller, rotor blade, and tailplane are all aerofoils.

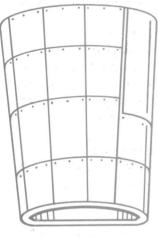

Aerofoil

Aileron
A moveable surface hinged to the trailing edge of a plane's wing used to control roll.

Airspeed indicator
An instrument that measures the speed of the aircraft when in flight.

Air-traffic control
The ground-based system that directs the movement of aircraft.

Altimeter
The instrument that records the height at which an aircraft is flying.

Autopilot
An electronic device that automatically maintains an aircraft in steady flight.

Biplane
An aeroplane with two sets of wings, one fixed above the other.

Bogie
The wheeled truck on the main landing leg.

Bulkhead
A solid partition that separates one part of an aeroplane from another.

Cantilever
A beam or other structure that is supported at one end only.

Cockpit
The compartment in a small aircraft that houses the pilot and crew.

Control surface
A moveable surface which, when moved, changes the aircraft's angle or direction of flight.

Co-pilot
The second pilot.

Delta wing
A triangular or near-triangular shaped wing with the trailing edge forming the flat base of the triangle. Concorde has delta wings.

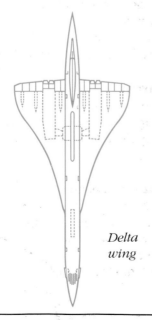

Delta wing

Drag
The resistance of the air to moving objects.

Elevator
A control surface hinged to the back of the tailplane that controls climb and descent.

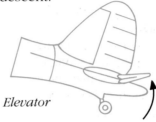

Elevator

Fin
The fixed vertical surface of a plane's tail unit that controls roll and yaw.

Flap
A surface hinged to the trailing edge of the wings which can be lowered partially to increase lift or fully to increase drag.

Flight deck
The crew compartment in a cabin aircraft.

Flight recorder
A crash-proof device that continually notes the speed, height, control-surface position, and other important aspects of an aeroplane in flight.

Flying boat
An aeroplane that can land and take off from water on its boat-shaped hull.

Flying wires
The wires of a non-cantilever wing which take the load of the wing in flight.

Fuselage
The body of an aircraft.

Galley
The compartment where food and drink are stored and prepared during a flight.

Glidepath
The sloping course along which an aircraft comes to land.

Gyro compass
A non-magnetic compass that indicates true north.

Inertial navigation system
A system that continuous measures changes in an aeroplane's speed and direction and feeds the information into a computer that works out the aircraft's precise position.

Instrument landing system
A system for guiding the pilot when landing in po visibility by means of two sets of radio beams transmitted from the ground alongside the runway.

Jet engine
An engine that draws in air, burns fuel in it, and emits a stream of hot gas that creates the thrust tha propels the aircraft forwards.

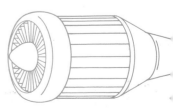

Jet engine

...ading edge
...aerofoil's front edge.

...ft
...e force generated by an
...rofoil when it is at 90
...grees to the airstream
...wing past it.

...ch 1
...e speed of sound
...193km/h [741mph]).

...agnetic compass
...instrument that contains
...magnetized needle that
...ways settles pointing to
...gnetic north.

...tch
...e up and down
...ovement of the nose
...d tail of an aircraft.
...ch is controlled by
...evators on the tailplane.

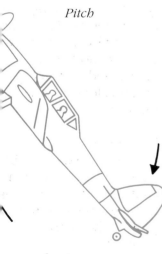
Pitch

...wer plant
...aircraft's engine or
...gines.

Propeller
The engine-driven rotating
blades that create the
thrust that pushes an
aircraft forwards.

Propeller

Radar
Radio **D**etection **and**
Ranging: the navigation
system that uses beams of
directed radio waves to
locate objects.

Radome
The protective covering
that houses radar antenna,
made from a material that
allows radar waves to pass
through it.

Reverse pitch
The way an aeroplane's
propeller blades are set so
that they exert a backward
thrust to slow the aircraft
after landing.

Reverse thrust
The effect caused by
deflecting a jet forward
so that it produces a
backward thrust that slows
the aeroplane after it lands.

Roll
The tilting, sideways
motion of an aeroplane.
Roll is controlled by the
wing ailerons.

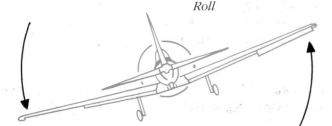
Roll

Rudder
The moveable control
surface hinged to the
rear of the tailfin that
controls yaw.

Slat
An extra, small moveable
surface fitted to the leading
edge of an aerofoil to
increase lift.

Slot
The gap between the slat
and the main aerofoil
surface.

Span
The distance from wingtip
to wingtip.

Spoiler
The control surface of an
aircraft's wings that
disturbs air-flow over the
wing and destroys lift. In
use they increase drag and
slow the aircraft.

Supersonic aircraft
Planes that fly at speeds
greater than Mach 1.

Tailplane
The horizontal aerofoil
surface of the tail unit that
provides stability along the
length of the aircraft. It
may be fixed or adjustable.

Thrust
The force generated by
propellers or jet flow that
propels a plane through
the air.

Thrust reversers
The parts of the engine
that deflect exhaust gases
forwards to slow
the aircraft
on landing.

Trailing edge
An aerofoil's rear edge.

Turbofan
A jet engine in which the
bulk of the air intake
bypasses the turbine and is
discharged as a cold jet.

Turbojet
A jet engine in which the
entire air intake passes
through the combustion
chamber and is discharged
as a hot jet.

Turboprop
A gas-turbine engine that
drives a propeller.

VTOL
Vertical **T**ake-**O**ff and
Landing.

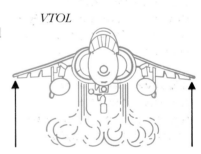
VTOL

Wing
The principal supporting
surface on both sides
of an aircraft.

Yaw
The swivelling movement
to right and left which can
be controlled by the
rudder on the tailfin.

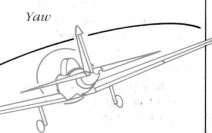
Yaw

INDEX

A

airliner, first, 8
anti-aircraft/submarine
    missiles, 24, 25

B

Battle of Britain, 13
Boeing
    314, 10-11
    747, 20-21
    747-400, 20
    747F, 21
    747SP, 20
    B-17, 14-15
    B-17G, 14
bombardiers, 14
bomber aeroplanes
    Boeing B-17,
    14-15
    Hawker Harrier,
    24-25
bombs, 14, 24

C

C-130 Hercules, 16-19
C-130H Hercules, 18
cannons, 12
cargo
    Boeing 314, 11
    Boeing 747, 21
    C-130H-30
    Hercules, 18
Clippers, 10, 11
cluster bombs, 24
cockpit
    Boeing 314, 10
    Boeing B-17, 14
    C-130 Hercules,
    16
    Handley Page
    H.P. 42, 9
    Spitfire, 13
    Piper PA-31, 23
Concorde, 26-27
Crew
    Boeing 314, 10
    Boeing 747, 20
    C-130 Hercules,
    16
Croydon Aerodrome
    (London), 8

E

ejection seat, 25
engines
    Allison T56-1A, 17
    Griffin, 12
    on Handley Page
    H.P. 42, 9
    on Hawker
    Harrier, 24
    Rolls-Royce
    Merlin, 12
    Rolls-Royce
    Pegasus, 24
    Rolls-Royce
    turbojet, 26
    Wright Cyclone,
    14
    Wright GR-2600, 11

F

Falklands War, 25
fighter aeroplanes
    Fokker Dr. 1, 6-7
    Fokker *Eindecker*,
    6
    Spitfire, 12-13
flight deck
    Boeing 747, 20
    Concorde, 26
flying boats, 10
Flying Fortress, 14-15
flying tankers, 17
Fokker Dr. 1, 6-7
Fokker *Eindecker*, 6
fuselage
    Handley Page
    H.P. 42, 9

G

galleys
    Concorde, 26
    Handley Page
    H.P. 42, 9
guns *see* machine guns

H

Handley Page H.P. 42, 8-9
Harrier, 24-25
Hawker Harrier, 24-25
Hercules, 16-19

I

Instrument panel
    Piper Chieftain
    PA-31, 23
    Spitfire, 13
interrupter gear, 7

J

Jumbo Jets, 20

L

landing gear/wheels
    Boeing 747, 21
    Concorde, 27
    Piper Chieftain
    PA-31, 22
light aircraft, 22
Lockheed C-130 Hercules,
    16-19
long-distance flights,
    14, 20

M

Mach 1, 27
machine guns
    Boeing B-17, 14
    Fokker Dr. 1, 6-7
    Spitfire, 12

P

passenger aeroplanes
    Boeing 747, 20-21
    Concorde, 26-27
    Handley Page
    H.P. 42, 8-9
passenger facilities on
    board
    Boeing 314, 10
    Boeing 747, 21
    Concorde, 26
    Handley Page
    H.P. 42, 9
    Piper Chieftain
    PA-31, 23
Piper Chieftain PA-31,
    22-23
propellers
    C-130 Hercules, 17
    Fokker Dr. 1, 6
    Spitfire, 12

R

radar, 16
Red Baron, 7
refuelling in mid-air, 17
Richthofen, Baron
    Manfred von, 7

S

Schneider Trophy race, 12
Sea Harrier, 24, 25
service area
    Handley Page
    H.P. 42, 9
speed
    Boeing 314, 11
    Boeing 747, 20
    Boeing B-17, 14
    Concorde, 27
    C-130 Hercules, 17
    Spitfire, 13
speed of sound, 27
Spitfire, 12-13
supersonic aircraft, 26

T

tailgunners, 15
triplanes, 6-7

V

VTOL (Vertical Take-Off
    and Landing), 24

W

waistgunners, 15
wide-bodied aeroplanes,
wings
    Fokker Dr. 1, 6
    Handley Page
    H.P. 42, 8

Acknowledgemen

Dorling Kindersley would li
to thank the following peop
who helped in the preparati
of this book:

Constance Novis for editorial
support
Lynn Bresler for the index
Boeing International
Corporation
Additional artwork by Brihton
Illustration (pages 28-29)
Line artworks by John See

LOOK INSIDE
CROSS-SECTIONS
PLANES

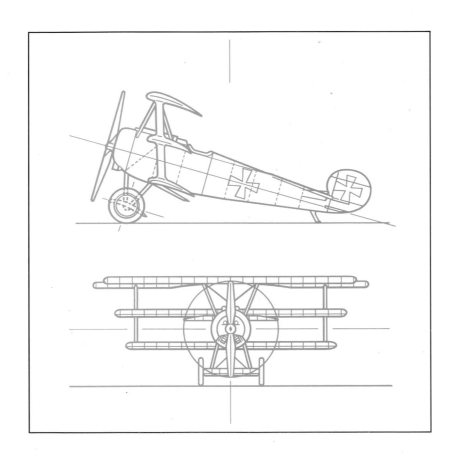